Gift lo

DATE	GIFT DESCRIPTION	GIVEN BY	THANK YOU NOTICE SENT

Gift log

Date	Gift Description	Given By	Thank You Notice Sent

Gift log

DATE	GIFT DESCRIPTION	GIVEN BY	THANK YOU NOTICE SENT

Gift log

Date	Gift Description	Given By	Thank You Notice Sent

Gift log

Date	Gift Description	Given By	Thank You Notice Sent

Gift log

DATE	GIFT DESCRIPTION	GIVEN BY	THANK YOU NOTICE SENT

Gift log

Date	Gift Description	Given By	Thank You Notice Sent

Gift log

Date	Gift Description	Given By	Thank You Notice Sent

Gift log

Date	Gift Description	Given By	Thank You Notice Sent

Gift log

Date	Gift Description	Given By	Thank You Notice Sent

Gift log

Date	Gift Description	Given By	Thank You Notice Sent

Gift log

Date	Gift Description	Given By	Thank You Notice Sent

Gift log

Date	Gift Description	Given By	Thank You Notice Sent

Gift log

DATE	GIFT DESCRIPTION	GIVEN BY	THANK YOU NOTICE SENT

Gift log

Date	Gift Description	Given By	Thank You Notice Sent

Gift log

Date	Gift Description	Given By	Thank You Notice Sent

Gift log

DATE	GIFT DESCRIPTION	GIVEN BY	THANK YOU NOTICE SENT

Gift log

Date	Gift Description	Given By	Thank You Notice Sent

Gift log

Date	Gift Description	Given By	Thank You Notice Sent

Gift log

Date	Gift Description	Given By	Thank You Notice Sent

Gift log

Date	Gift Description	Given By	Thank You Notice Sent

Gift log

Date	Gift Description	Given By	Thank You Notice Sent

Gift log

Date	Gift Description	Given By	Thank You Notice Sent

Gift log

Date	Gift Description	Given By	Thank You Notice Sent

Gift log

Date	Gift Description	Given By	Thank You Notice Sent

Gift log

Date	Gift Description	Given By	Thank You Notice Sent

Gift log

Date	Gift Description	Given By	Thank You Notice Sent

Gift log

Date	Gift Description	Given By	Thank You Notice Sent

Gift log

Date	Gift Description	Given By	Thank You Notice Sent

Gift log

Date	Gift Description	Given By	Thank You Notice Sent

Gift log

Date	Gift Description	Given By	Thank You Notice Sent

Gift log

Date	Gift Description	Given By	Thank You Notice Sent

Gift log

Date	Gift Description	Given By	Thank You Notice Sent

Gift log

Date	Gift Description	Given By	Thank You Notice Sent

Gift log

Date	Gift Description	Given By	Thank You Notice Sent

Gift log

Date	Gift Description	Given By	Thank You Notice Sent

Gift log

Date	Gift Description	Given By	Thank You Notice Sent

Gift log

Date	Gift Description	Given By	Thank You Notice Sent

Gift log

Date	Gift Description	Given By	Thank You Notice Sent

Gift log

Date	Gift Description	Given By	Thank You Notice Sent

Gift log

Date	Gift Description	Given By	Thank You Notice Sent

Gift log

Date	Gift Description	Given By	Thank You Notice Sent

Gift log

Date	Gift Description	Given By	Thank You Notice Sent

Contacts

NAME	
ADDRESS	
HOME NO.	CELL NO.
EMAIL	
NOTES	

NAME	
ADDRESS	
HOME NO.	CELL NO.
EMAIL	
NOTES	

NAME	
ADDRESS	
HOME NO.	CELL NO.
EMAIL	
NOTES	

Contacts

NAME	
ADDRESS	
HOME NO.	**CELL NO.**
EMAIL	
NOTES	

NAME	
ADDRESS	
HOME NO.	**CELL NO.**
EMAIL	
NOTES	

NAME	
ADDRESS	
HOME NO.	**CELL NO.**
EMAIL	
NOTES	

Contacts

NAME	
ADDRESS	
HOME NO.	**CELL NO.**
EMAIL	
NOTES	

NAME	
ADDRESS	
HOME NO.	**CELL NO.**
EMAIL	
NOTES	

NAME	
ADDRESS	
HOME NO.	**CELL NO.**
EMAIL	
NOTES	

Contacts

NAME	
ADDRESS	
HOME NO.	**CELL NO.**
EMAIL	
NOTES	

NAME	
ADDRESS	
HOME NO.	**CELL NO.**
EMAIL	
NOTES	

NAME	
ADDRESS	
HOME NO.	**CELL NO.**
EMAIL	
NOTES	

Contacts

NAME	
ADDRESS	
HOME NO.	**CELL NO.**
EMAIL	
NOTES	

NAME	
ADDRESS	
HOME NO.	**CELL NO.**
EMAIL	
NOTES	

NAME	
ADDRESS	
HOME NO.	**CELL NO.**
EMAIL	
NOTES	

Contacts

NAME	
ADDRESS	
HOME NO.	CELL NO.
EMAIL	
NOTES	

NAME	
ADDRESS	
HOME NO.	CELL NO.
EMAIL	
NOTES	

NAME	
ADDRESS	
HOME NO.	CELL NO.
EMAIL	
NOTES	

NAME	
ADDRESS	
HOME NO.	**CELL NO.**
EMAIL	
NOTES	

NAME	
ADDRESS	
HOME NO.	**CELL NO.**
EMAIL	
NOTES	

NAME	
ADDRESS	
HOME NO.	**CELL NO.**
EMAIL	
NOTES	

Contacts

NAME	
ADDRESS	
HOME NO.	**CELL NO.**
EMAIL	
NOTES	

NAME	
ADDRESS	
HOME NO.	**CELL NO.**
EMAIL	
NOTES	

NAME	
ADDRESS	
HOME NO.	**CELL NO.**
EMAIL	
NOTES	

Contacts

NAME	
ADDRESS	
HOME NO.	**CELL NO.**
EMAIL	
NOTES	

NAME	
ADDRESS	
HOME NO.	**CELL NO.**
EMAIL	
NOTES	

NAME	
ADDRESS	
HOME NO.	**CELL NO.**
EMAIL	
NOTES	

Contacts

NAME	
ADDRESS	
HOME NO.	**CELL NO.**
EMAIL	
NOTES	

NAME	
ADDRESS	
HOME NO.	**CELL NO.**
EMAIL	
NOTES	

NAME	
ADDRESS	
HOME NO.	**CELL NO.**
EMAIL	
NOTES	

Contacts

NAME	
ADDRESS	
HOME NO.	CELL NO.
EMAIL	
NOTES	

NAME	
ADDRESS	
HOME NO.	CELL NO.
EMAIL	
NOTES	

NAME	
ADDRESS	
HOME NO.	CELL NO.
EMAIL	
NOTES	

Contacts

NAME	
ADDRESS	
HOME NO.	**CELL NO.**
EMAIL	
NOTES	

NAME	
ADDRESS	
HOME NO.	**CELL NO.**
EMAIL	
NOTES	

NAME	
ADDRESS	
HOME NO.	**CELL NO.**
EMAIL	
NOTES	

Contacts

NAME	
ADDRESS	
HOME NO.	**CELL NO.**
EMAIL	
NOTES	

NAME	
ADDRESS	
HOME NO.	**CELL NO.**
EMAIL	
NOTES	

NAME	
ADDRESS	
HOME NO.	**CELL NO.**
EMAIL	
NOTES	

Contacts

NAME	
ADDRESS	
HOME NO.	CELL NO.
EMAIL	
NOTES	

NAME	
ADDRESS	
HOME NO.	CELL NO.
EMAIL	
NOTES	

NAME	
ADDRESS	
HOME NO.	CELL NO.
EMAIL	
NOTES	

Contacts

NAME	
ADDRESS	
HOME NO.	**CELL NO.**
EMAIL	
NOTES	

NAME	
ADDRESS	
HOME NO.	**CELL NO.**
EMAIL	
NOTES	

NAME	
ADDRESS	
HOME NO.	**CELL NO.**
EMAIL	
NOTES	

Contacts

NAME	
ADDRESS	
HOME NO.	**CELL NO.**
EMAIL	
NOTES	

NAME	
ADDRESS	
HOME NO.	**CELL NO.**
EMAIL	
NOTES	

NAME	
ADDRESS	
HOME NO.	**CELL NO.**
EMAIL	
NOTES	

Contacts

NAME	
ADDRESS	
HOME NO.	**CELL NO.**
EMAIL	
NOTES	

NAME	
ADDRESS	
HOME NO.	**CELL NO.**
EMAIL	
NOTES	

NAME	
ADDRESS	
HOME NO.	**CELL NO.**
EMAIL	
NOTES	

Contacts

NAME	
ADDRESS	
HOME NO.	**CELL NO.**
EMAIL	
NOTES	

NAME	
ADDRESS	
HOME NO.	**CELL NO.**
EMAIL	
NOTES	

NAME	
ADDRESS	
HOME NO.	**CELL NO.**
EMAIL	
NOTES	

Contacts

NAME	
ADDRESS	
HOME NO.	**CELL NO.**
EMAIL	
NOTES	

NAME	
ADDRESS	
HOME NO.	**CELL NO.**
EMAIL	
NOTES	

NAME	
ADDRESS	
HOME NO.	**CELL NO.**
EMAIL	
NOTES	

Contacts

NAME	
ADDRESS	
HOME NO.	**CELL NO.**
EMAIL	
NOTES	

NAME	
ADDRESS	
HOME NO.	**CELL NO.**
EMAIL	
NOTES	

NAME	
ADDRESS	
HOME NO.	**CELL NO.**
EMAIL	
NOTES	

Contacts

NAME	
ADDRESS	
HOME NO.	**CELL NO.**
EMAIL	
NOTES	

NAME	
ADDRESS	
HOME NO.	**CELL NO.**
EMAIL	
NOTES	

NAME	
ADDRESS	
HOME NO.	**CELL NO.**
EMAIL	
NOTES	

Contacts

NAME	
ADDRESS	
HOME NO.	**CELL NO.**
EMAIL	
NOTES	

NAME	
ADDRESS	
HOME NO.	**CELL NO.**
EMAIL	
NOTES	

NAME	
ADDRESS	
HOME NO.	**CELL NO.**
EMAIL	
NOTES	

Contacts

NAME	
ADDRESS	
HOME NO.	**CELL NO.**
EMAIL	
NOTES	

NAME	
ADDRESS	
HOME NO.	**CELL NO.**
EMAIL	
NOTES	

NAME	
ADDRESS	
HOME NO.	**CELL NO.**
EMAIL	
NOTES	

Contacts

NAME	
ADDRESS	
HOME NO.	**CELL NO.**
EMAIL	
NOTES	

NAME	
ADDRESS	
HOME NO.	**CELL NO.**
EMAIL	
NOTES	

NAME	
ADDRESS	
HOME NO.	**CELL NO.**
EMAIL	
NOTES	

Contacts

NAME	
ADDRESS	
HOME NO.	**CELL NO.**
EMAIL	
NOTES	

NAME	
ADDRESS	
HOME NO.	**CELL NO.**
EMAIL	
NOTES	

NAME	
ADDRESS	
HOME NO.	**CELL NO.**
EMAIL	
NOTES	

Contacts

NAME	
ADDRESS	
HOME No.	**CELL No.**
EMAIL	
NOTES	

NAME	
ADDRESS	
HOME No.	**CELL No.**
EMAIL	
NOTES	

NAME	
ADDRESS	
HOME No.	**CELL No.**
EMAIL	
NOTES	

Contacts

NAME	
ADDRESS	
HOME NO.	**CELL NO.**
EMAIL	
NOTES	

NAME	
ADDRESS	
HOME NO.	**CELL NO.**
EMAIL	
NOTES	

NAME	
ADDRESS	
HOME NO.	**CELL NO.**
EMAIL	
NOTES	

Contacts

NAME	
ADDRESS	
HOME NO.	**CELL NO.**
EMAIL	
NOTES	

NAME	
ADDRESS	
HOME NO.	**CELL NO.**
EMAIL	
NOTES	

NAME	
ADDRESS	
HOME NO.	**CELL NO.**
EMAIL	
NOTES	

Contacts

NAME	
ADDRESS	
HOME NO.	**CELL NO.**
EMAIL	
NOTES	

NAME	
ADDRESS	
HOME NO.	**CELL NO.**
EMAIL	
NOTES	

NAME	
ADDRESS	
HOME NO.	**CELL NO.**
EMAIL	
NOTES	

Contacts

NAME	
ADDRESS	

HOME NO.	**CELL NO.**
EMAIL	
NOTES	

NAME	
ADDRESS	

HOME NO.	**CELL NO.**
EMAIL	
NOTES	

NAME	
ADDRESS	

HOME NO.	**CELL NO.**
EMAIL	
NOTES	

Contacts

NAME	
ADDRESS	
HOME NO.	**CELL NO.**
EMAIL	
NOTES	

NAME	
ADDRESS	
HOME NO.	**CELL NO.**
EMAIL	
NOTES	

NAME	
ADDRESS	
HOME NO.	**CELL NO.**
EMAIL	
NOTES	

Contacts

NAME	
ADDRESS	
HOME NO.	**CELL NO.**
EMAIL	
NOTES	

NAME	
ADDRESS	
HOME NO.	**CELL NO.**
EMAIL	
NOTES	

NAME	
ADDRESS	
HOME NO.	**CELL NO.**
EMAIL	
NOTES	

Contacts

NAME	
ADDRESS	
HOME NO.	**CELL NO.**
EMAIL	
NOTES	

NAME	
ADDRESS	
HOME NO.	**CELL NO.**
EMAIL	
NOTES	

NAME	
ADDRESS	
HOME NO.	**CELL NO.**
EMAIL	
NOTES	

Contacts

NAME	
ADDRESS	
HOME NO.	**CELL NO.**
EMAIL	
NOTES	

NAME	
ADDRESS	
HOME NO.	**CELL NO.**
EMAIL	
NOTES	

NAME	
ADDRESS	
HOME NO.	**CELL NO.**
EMAIL	
NOTES	

Contacts

NAME	
ADDRESS	
HOME No.	**CELL No.**
EMAIL	
NOTES	

NAME	
ADDRESS	
HOME No.	**CELL No.**
EMAIL	
NOTES	

NAME	
ADDRESS	
HOME No.	**CELL No.**
EMAIL	
NOTES	

Contosts

NAME	
ADDRESS	
HOME NO.	**CELL NO.**
EMAIL	
NOTES	

NAME	
ADDRESS	
HOME NO.	**CELL NO.**
EMAIL	
NOTES	

NAME	
ADDRESS	
HOME NO.	**CELL NO.**
EMAIL	
NOTES	

Contacts

NAME	
ADDRESS	
HOME NO.	**CELL NO.**
EMAIL	
NOTES	

NAME	
ADDRESS	
HOME NO.	**CELL NO.**
EMAIL	
NOTES	

NAME	
ADDRESS	
HOME NO.	**CELL NO.**
EMAIL	
NOTES	

Contacts

NAME	
ADDRESS	
HOME NO.	**CELL NO.**
EMAIL	
NOTES	

NAME	
ADDRESS	
HOME NO.	**CELL NO.**
EMAIL	
NOTES	

NAME	
ADDRESS	
HOME NO.	**CELL NO.**
EMAIL	
NOTES	

Contacts

NAME	
ADDRESS	
HOME NO.	**CELL NO.**
EMAIL	
NOTES	

NAME	
ADDRESS	
HOME NO.	**CELL NO.**
EMAIL	
NOTES	

NAME	
ADDRESS	
HOME NO.	**CELL NO.**
EMAIL	
NOTES	

Contacts

NAME	
ADDRESS	
HOME NO.	**CELL NO.**
EMAIL	
NOTES	

NAME	
ADDRESS	
HOME NO.	**CELL NO.**
EMAIL	
NOTES	

NAME	
ADDRESS	
HOME NO.	**CELL NO.**
EMAIL	
NOTES	

Contacts

NAME	
ADDRESS	
HOME NO.	**CELL NO.**
EMAIL	
NOTES	

NAME	
ADDRESS	
HOME NO.	**CELL NO.**
EMAIL	
NOTES	

NAME	
ADDRESS	
HOME NO.	**CELL NO.**
EMAIL	
NOTES	

#

NAME	
ADDRESS	
HOME NO.	**CELL NO.**
EMAIL	
NOTES	

NAME	
ADDRESS	
HOME NO.	**CELL NO.**
EMAIL	
NOTES	

NAME	
ADDRESS	
HOME NO.	**CELL NO.**
EMAIL	
NOTES	

Contacts

NAME	
ADDRESS	
HOME NO.	**CELL NO.**
EMAIL	
NOTES	

NAME	
ADDRESS	
HOME NO.	**CELL NO.**
EMAIL	
NOTES	

NAME	
ADDRESS	
HOME NO.	**CELL NO.**
EMAIL	
NOTES	

Contacts

NAME	
ADDRESS	
HOME NO.	**CELL NO.**
EMAIL	
NOTES	

NAME	
ADDRESS	
HOME NO.	**CELL NO.**
EMAIL	
NOTES	

NAME	
ADDRESS	
HOME NO.	**CELL NO.**
EMAIL	
NOTES	

Contacts

NAME	
ADDRESS	
HOME NO.	**CELL NO.**
EMAIL	
NOTES	

NAME	
ADDRESS	
HOME NO.	**CELL NO.**
EMAIL	
NOTES	

NAME	
ADDRESS	
HOME NO.	**CELL NO.**
EMAIL	
NOTES	

Contacts

NAME	
ADDRESS	
HOME NO.	**CELL NO.**
EMAIL	
NOTES	

NAME	
ADDRESS	
HOME NO.	**CELL NO.**
EMAIL	
NOTES	

NAME	
ADDRESS	
HOME NO.	**CELL NO.**
EMAIL	
NOTES	

Contacts

NAME	
ADDRESS	
HOME NO.	**CELL NO.**
EMAIL	
NOTES	

NAME	
ADDRESS	
HOME NO.	**CELL NO.**
EMAIL	
NOTES	

NAME	
ADDRESS	
HOME NO.	**CELL NO.**
EMAIL	
NOTES	

Contacts

NAME	
ADDRESS	
HOME NO.	**CELL NO.**
EMAIL	
NOTES	

NAME	
ADDRESS	
HOME NO.	**CELL NO.**
EMAIL	
NOTES	

NAME	
ADDRESS	
HOME NO.	**CELL NO.**
EMAIL	
NOTES	

Contacts

NAME	
ADDRESS	
HOME NO.	**CELL NO.**
EMAIL	
NOTES	

NAME	
ADDRESS	
HOME NO.	**CELL NO.**
EMAIL	
NOTES	

NAME	
ADDRESS	
HOME NO.	**CELL NO.**
EMAIL	
NOTES	

Notes

Notes

Notes

Notes

Notes

Notes

Notes

Notes

Notes

Made in the USA
Las Vegas, NV
23 August 2021